Suzuki®

Cello School
Volume 5
Piano Accompaniment
Revised Edition

CONTENTS

ISBN 0-87487-270-7

INTRODUCTION

FOR THE STUDENT: This material is part of the worldwide Suzuki Method of teaching. Companion recordings should be used with these publications. In addition, there are cello part books that go along with this material.

FOR THE TEACHER: In order to be an effective Suzuki teacher, a great deal of ongoing education is required. Your national Suzuki association provides this for its membership. Teachers are encouraged to become members of their national Suzuki associations and maintain a teacher training schedule, in order to remain current, via institutes, short-term programs, and long-term programs. You are also encouraged to join the International Suzuki Association.

FOR THE PARENT: Credentials are essential for any teacher you choose. We recommend you ask your teacher for his or her credentials, especially those relating to training in the Suzuki Method. The Suzuki Method experience should be a positive one, where there exists a wonderful, fostering relationship among child, parent, and teacher. So choosing the right teacher is of the utmost importance.

In order to obtain more information about the Suzuki Association in your region please contact:

International Suzuki Association USA Office
212 S. Cottonwood Dr.
Richardson, TX 75080
www.internationalsuzuki.org

Under the guidance of Dr. Suzuki since 1978, the editing of the Suzuki Cello School is a continuing cooperative effort of the International Suzuki Association Cello Committee.

Sonata in E minor

Op. 14, No. 5

Antonio Vivaldi
(1678-1741)

Allegro
mf
p
cresc.

15
p
cresc.
f
p
cresc.
f
mp
mf
mp
mf
22
25
f
f

29
mf
cresc.
mf
cresc.
32
mf
mf
34
37
cresc.
f
cresc.
f

Largo
mf_p
mf_p
3
mf
mf
6
mf
mp
mf
mf
mp
mf
(8)
cresc.
f
cresc.
f

Allegro
mf
mf
10
mf
p
mf
p
19
mf
cresc.
mf
cresc.
28
mf
cresc.
mf
cresc.

37
mf
46
p
54
cresc.
mf
p
62
f
p
mf
cresc. e rall.

Danse Rustique

Op. 20, No. 5

William Henry Squire
(1871-1963)

27
33
mf
p
39
45
cresc.
f
cresc.
f

51
p
mf
8va
58
cresc.
f
65
70

76
82
p
p
mf
87
8va
p
p
92
mf
mf

97
mf
p
102
107
cresc.
cresc.
f
f
112
mf
mf
p
p
mf
mf

117
p
mf
p
122
cresc.
f
cresc.
f

Arioso

Johann Sebastian Bach
(1685-1750)

cresc.
cresc.
cresc.
molto rit.
molto rit.

Rondo

from the Concerto No. 4, Op. 65

(excerpt)

Georg Goltermann
(1824-1898)

35
44
p
53
cresc.
mf cresc.
cresc.
62
f cresc.
mf
ff
cresc.

71
80
89
99

108
molto grazioso ed affettuoso
mf
p
118
128
138
cresc.
f con passione
cresc.
mf

150
ff
rall.
a tempo
a tempo
rall.
espress.
p
160
mf
p
168
mf
p
176
f

184
mf
cresc.
ff pesante
cresc.
mf pesante
p
193
Piu animato
rit.
dim.
mf
rit.
dim.
p espress.
202
210
cresc.
f

219
226
brilliante
mf
cresc.
mf
cresc.
234
ff
f
241
ff
ff